FISHING

FISHING

by Jerolyn Ann Nentl

Library of Congress Catalog Card Number: 80-10490

International Standard Book Number: 0-89686-070-1

Designed and Produced by - Randal M. Heise

Crestwood House, Inc., Mankato, Minnesota 56001

Edited by - Dr. Howard Schroeder
Prof. in Reading and Language Arts
Dept. of Elementary Education
Mankato State University

Our special thanks to the **In-Fisherman** magazine with whose help this book was effectively illustrated.

Library of Congress
Cataloging in Publication Data

Nentl, Jerolyn Ann.
  Fishing.

  (Back to nature sports)
  SUMMARY: Introduces fishing, including lures, bait, and casting.
  1. Fishing--Juvenile literature. (1. Fishing) I. Schroeder, Howard. II. Title. III. Series.
  SH445.N46   799.1   80-10490
  ISBN 0-89686-070-1

Joe sat as still as he could in the boat, bending over his fishing rod. He knew fish were easily scared by any sudden noise or movement. The water of the lake lapped gently against the side of the boat. There was hardly another sound, except for a splash now and then. It was difficult to stay awake. Even sitting on the hard seat in the boat was not helping much. Joe had baited his hook and cast it into the water. There was nothing more to do now until he felt a tug on his line. He knew the fish would soon be up from the depths of the lake looking for something to eat. The early morning was one of their favorite feeding times. Keeping an eye on his bobber, Joe huddled a little deeper into his jacket. Early morning fog still covered the lake, and it was chilly. Joe liked this part of fishing. He could daydream all he wanted, and no one would accuse him of being lazy. His sister, Jane, was sitting quietly behind him on the other seat in the boat. On the shore their parents were still asleep in the tent.

Fish are never really caught until they're in the boat.

A slight tug on the line caught Joe's attention! His bobber had been jerked below the water. Then he felt a second tug, a little stronger than the first. Joe tightened his grip on the fishing rod. A fish was nibbling on his bait! When he felt the third tug, he lifted his rod sharply to set the hook. He felt the fish pull away, and he let it run with the line. Playing a fish was exciting! It was a contest between him and the fish.

The fish pulled hard on the line and jumped. When it was tired, Joe reeled it toward the boat. Raising the tip of his rod, he grabbed it as it came out of the water. It was a nice two-pound largemouth bass. Joe turned around to show his catch to his sister, but she was too busy to admire it. She had a fish at the end of her line, too. Joe settled back to watch his sister land her catch. It had been a good morning. All they had to do now was row ashore, clean their catch, and get out the frying pan!

It is always a thrill to catch a fish. The size of the fish nor the number caught is not important. It is the contest between fisherman and fish that keeps people coming back to their favorite lake or stream year after year. With each fish, there is a new challenge. Each lake or stream is different, too. Today there is also a wide choice of rods and reels, lines and lures which help make the sport so interesting.

Just as with hunting, people fished to feed themselves long before they ever fished for fun. Drawings of hunters with fish and animals have been discovered on the walls of caves that are thousands of years old. Today, fishing is a sport enjoyed by people of all ages in every country of the world. Sometimes people call fishing "angling."

This drawing of a Egyptian spearing fish is thousands of years old.

The first fishing lines were only vines or braided grass. Later, braided horsetail hairs and natural fibers like linen and silk were used. Bait was tied to the end of the line to attract a fish. Adding a pole was the next step. With a pole, an angler, or fisherman, could reach out farther from the bank, across bushes and tall grass, into deeper water. The first poles were simple sticks. These early fishing lines were tied to the end of poles. An angler could not do much with them except lower them into the water. During the 1600's, a wire ring or loop was added at the end of the pole and the line was threaded through it. More line could be let out this way, and anglers could cast their bait farther out into the water. The next invention was a spool or "winder" on which to store the extra line. The first spools were made of wood and were very difficult to control. These spools were the first reels. They appeared in Europe in the 1800's.

Izaak Walton is called the father of modern fishing. He wrote a
book called "The Complete Angler" in 1653. Methods described in
his book are still used today.

This old photo shows a good day's catch.

The first fishing hooks came from things found in nature: a thorn from a bush, the curved beak of an eagle or a hawk's claw. Later, hooks were made of wood and stone. They were also made of bone, perhaps carved from the horn of a deer or the tooth of a whale. Today's fish hooks come in many sizes, lengths, weights and finishes. There is no one all-around hook that is good for all kinds of fishing. There are too many different kinds and sizes of fish and ways of catching them. One estimate is that there may be 75,000 different types of fish hooks today! The most popular are the single hook and the treble hook. Single hooks are used with bait or flies. The treble hook, which has three barbs, is used with lures and plugs.

Catching a fish with a hook and line is not always easy. Anglers must know where the fish are, and what kind of bait or lure to use. An angler's bait can be any food a fish will eat. The most popular baits for fresh-water fish are worms, minnows, and insects. Salt-water fish go for small crabs, squid, clams, and sea mussels. Lures are man-made, or artificial bait. There are six main kinds of lures: flies, spinners, spoons, plugs, jigs, and the new soft plastic baits.

Plastic Baits   **Flies**   **Spinner Bait**   **Jigs**

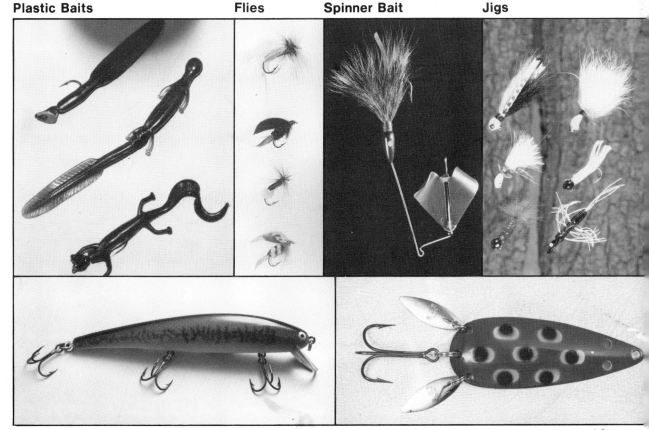

Plug   **Spoon**

Flies

A fly is a hook with small pieces of silk, hair, or feathers tied to it. It is made to look like a real fly or another insect. Flies can be made to float, or to be used beneath the surface. "Dry" flies stay on the surface, while "wet" flies will sink.

Spinners

A spinner is a metal blade that moves, or spins, as it is pulled through the water. The flash of the blade makes it look like a small fish as it swims.

Spoons

Spoons are pieces of metal shaped like a spoon. They are made so that they move unevenly through the water, looking like a wounded fish.

Plugs

Plugs are pieces of wood or plastic made to look like baitfish. They are made to move in a way that will attract a fish when they are pulled through the water. Some go deep in the water while others stay near, or on, the surface.

Soft Plastic Baits

This is the newest type of lure. The lures are made to look like the many things that fish eat.

Jigs

Jigs are probably the best all-around lure. To make them, a ball of lead is molded around the shaft of a hook. Then feathers, hair, or soft plastic bodies and "wigglies" can be added. They can be made to look like just about anything a fish would eat. To make them even more effective, you can add live bait or soft plastic baits to the hook.

Black crappie chases a jig.

It's a big thrill to catch a nice one.

Once they have chosen their bait or lure, anglers must know how to "rig," or tie, it to the line. Sometimes an angler will tie a thinner piece of line, called a "leader," to the main fishing line. The hook or lure and any sinkers or bobbers the angler is using are then tied to the leader. This tackle, connected to the main fishing line, is called the "terminal tackle."

Anglers must also know how to offer their bait or lure to the fish without scaring them away. Finally, they must know how to set the hook, play the fish, and land it. It also helps to know how to clean and cook fish!

It hasn't been proven, but some people believe that different stages of the moon effect the activity of fish.

The In-Fisherman magazine is a very informative magazine for people who take fishing seriously.

Some of this knowledge can be learned from reading books and magazines. Anglers can learn much by talking to other anglers. Most knowledge about fishing comes only with experience. By going fishing, anglers learn to "read" the water and weather. They learn how fish behave, too. The more anglers know about fish and their habits, the more fun they will have, and the more they may catch.

There are three main types of fish: fresh-water, salt-water, and "anadromous."

Fresh-water anglers can fish in small streams or large rivers, farm ponds or huge lakes. Trout is a fresh-water fish of rivers and streams. In ponds and lakes, most fresh-water anglers are after bass, walleye, and northern pike. They will also catch sunfish, bluegills, crappies, yellow perch, or bullheads (these are called "panfish.").

Salt-water anglers fish in the surf or "offshore" in the deeper waters of the oceans. Salt-water fish are al-

This boat is equipped for deep sea fishing.

ways on the move. This makes them more difficult to catch. The most popular salt-water game fish are flounder, black sea bass, perch, rockfish, porgy, billfish such as swordfish, snapper and sharks. The real trophies of salt-water sport fishing, however, are the big game fish. These include sailfish, swordfish, tuna, sharks and marlin. A fish like this may weigh one hundred to two thousand pounds! This kind of fishing requires special boats, equipment, and know-how.

The third type of fish, called "anadromous," live in both fresh and salt-water. The most popular fish of this kind is salmon. Steelhead trout, striped bass, shad, and sturgeon are also anadromous fish. These fish are usually caught in the rivers that empty into the ocean.

The simplest way to fish is to "stillfish." Anglers stay in one place to stillfish. They simply drop their baited hooks or lures into the water and wait for a fish to bite. Then the angler sets the hook and pulls in the catch. Like the name says, stillfishing is done in still or calm waters. If the waters are moving, it is called driftfishing. Stillfishing and driftfishing are often done from the bank of a river or stream, from piers, bridges, and jetties. They can also be done from a boat anchored out on a lake or in the ocean.

To stillfish or driftfish, an angler needs only basic equipment: a rod, line, bait or lures, sinkers, and bobbers. A reel is not needed, but having one makes the job of landing a catch easier.

Sinkers are special weights used to get the bait deeper in the water. Getting the bait or lure to the proper depth in the water is very important in any kind of fishing. Bobbers, or floats, keep the bait from sinking too far.

Former Governor of Minnesota, Wendell Anderson, pulls in a "keeper."

Trolling is very much like stillfishing and driftfishing. To troll, an angler lets out some line and trails it behind a boat that is moving very slowly. In salt-water fishing, anglers may scatter ground-up bait called "chum" behind their boats to attract the fish. This is called "chumming." Some anglers dislike trolling and chumming and do not consider it true sport fishing. Other anglers feel that these methods, because they take years to learn, are just as sporting as any other. It's just an honest difference of opinion.

Anglers, who want to see more action than what stillfishing, driftfishing, or trolling provide, can try casting and retrieving. Casting is simply throwing the bait or lure into the water. Retrieving is working the rod and reel so that the bait or lure will attract a fish as the angler reels in the line. If all the line has been retrieved without a bite, the angler tries again. A different lure can be used. The angler can cast to a different spot in the water or try fishing at a different depth, too. If an angler gets a strike on the first cast, the best thing to do is to cast to the same spot as quickly as possible and retrieve the line in the same way as before.

There are four ways of casting and retrieving. They are named after the four different types of rod and reel used: flycasting, bait casting, spinning and spin casting.

Fly Casting

Fly casting is a special kind of fishing using an artificial fly to attract the fish. Fly fishermen are usually after trout, salmon, or panfish. The fly rod is very lightweight and bends easily. It is usually seven to ten feet long. The reel on the fly rod is used only to store the line. It is not used during the cast. A fly fisherman "strips," or pulls, the line from the reel by hand, holding the slack in the hand during the cast, and sometimes during the retrieve.

Bait Casting

Bait casting uses live bait or lures. The angler casts and retrieves the bait or lure. The bait casting rod is five to six feet long, with the reel mounted on top near the handle. The reel has a spool that turns to let line out on the cast. Many casting reels have a "drag" device on them. This adjusts so that the line comes off the reel with the right amount of "tension." If it comes off too easily, it will tangle; if it is too tight it may break.

Spinning

Spinning gear combines features of the fly casting and the bait casting reels. A spinning rod is more limber and longer than a bait casting rod. However, it is not as flexible and long as a fly rod. The spool does not turn at any time during the cast. Instead, the line is pulled off the end of the spool by the weight of the lure as it is cast. During the retrieve, the line is rewound on the spool by a special device that winds the line onto the spool. The angler's forefinger helps control the amount of line used during the cast.

Spin Casting

Like the bait casting reel, the spin casting reel is mounted on top of the rod near the handle. Like the spinning reel, it has a spool that does not turn. Unlike the spinning reel, however, the spin casting spool is covered, or "closed-face." A push-button on top of the reel controls the amount of line used during a cast. It is sometimes called "a mechanical thumb." The spin casting rod, like the bait casting rod, is usually five to six feet long.

Spinning Rod & Reel   **Fly Casting Rod & Reel**

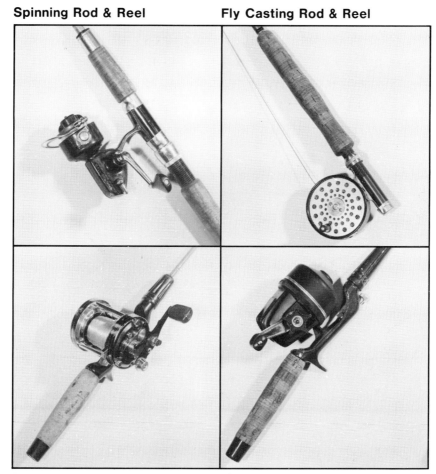

Bait Casting Rod & Reel   **Spin Casting Rod & Reel**

The one-handed, overhead cast is basic. Anglers will sometimes use both hands for more control if their hands are small, or if the rod is heavy. This type of cast is used in bait casting, spinning, and spin casting. An average cast might be twenty to sixty feet! The angler points the rod at the target, then raises the tip sharply but smoothly until the rod is straight up. The motion is with the wrist, not the elbow or the shoulder. The weight of the lure whips the line backwards over the angler's shoulder. This bends the rod. When the angler "feels" the line has straightened out, the rod is sharply brought forward. At the same time, the angler releases the line. Knowing the right time to release the line is called "timing."

Anglers can also cast to the side or with a backhand motion. This is done only if there is something like a bush or a tree in the way preventing an overhead cast. To cast properly and accurately, an angler must learn good wrist action and the right timing.

In the fly cast, all the action is done with the arm by bending the elbow. An angler's wrist does **not** bend. The fly fisherman lifts the tip of the rod sharply with one arm while the other hand controls slack line that has been pulled from the reel. The slack line loops up and over the angler's shoulder as the rod is brought up. When the angler "feels" that the slack line has straightened out, the rod is brought sharply forward. The weight of the line propels the fly to the target point on the water. Anglers hold many fly casting contests each year to see how far, and how close to the target they can cast. The world distance record for fly casting in 1979 was 201 feet!

Once a fish bites, anglers "play the fish" until it gets tired and can be landed. Playing the fish means keeping the right amount of tension, or pressure, on the line. To do this, the angler keeps the rod tip upright. This keeps the hook firmly in the fish and the angler stays in control of the action. The fish can swim, wiggle and jump all it wants, and it will not slip off the angler's hook. Too much pressure may cause the hook to tear out of the fish's mouth. The rod or line might break, too. Too little pressure lets the line go slack. With slack line, the fish can wiggle or jump loose of the hook. Knowing just how much pressure to apply comes with practice.

Landing the fish can be easy. Anglers usually try to grab their catch as it turns over on its side. If the fish is not completely tired out, the angler may choose to net or gaff it with a large hook when it gets close to the boat. Once the catch is landed, the fishing may be finished but the fun is not. Most anglers like to take pictures of themselves with their prize catches to show family and friends. "Fish stories" are told and retold for many years. Fish that anglers have caught themselves always seem to taste better, too.

It took all night, but these two brought home their limit. Some people will fish in any weather and at any time if the fish happen to be biting.

Anyone can go fishing. Anyone can get lucky and catch a fish. They might even catch two, three, or four fish. However, to catch fish regularly takes skill and knowledge. Smart anglers often follow these rules.

* Don't go near the water unless you know how to swim.
* Know how to operate your boat safely, and be considerate of other boaters.
* Know how to remove a hook from a fish, and be careful not to "hook" yourself or one of your partners.
* Fish only in season and with a license, if one is required in your area. Anglers should also follow the rules of their area regarding the size and number of fish allowed. An angler does not always need to catch the limit to have a good time.

To be successful, an angler must be fishing in the right place, at the right time, and with the right bait. It's easy, if an angler has learned to "think like a fish."